Original title:
Berry Bliss

Copyright © 2025 Creative Arts Management OÜ
All rights reserved.

Author: Liam Sterling
ISBN HARDBACK: 978-1-80586-242-0
ISBN PAPERBACK: 978-1-80586-714-2

Mosaic of Colors

Red, blue, and a little green,
They dangle from branches, a vibrant scene.
Plucking them off, with giggles and glee,
"Just one more" turns into a whole spree.

Juicy dribbles stain my shirt,
A splash of happiness, no one gets hurt.
I slip on a leaf, oh what a twist,
But these fruits of delight? They're too good to miss!

Sugary Serenades

A chorus of sweetness, they sing on a vine,
In the patch, we dance, sipping lemonade fine.
With each juicy bite, my worries float by,
I'll trade all my socks for a slice of the sky.

Fingers sticky, laughter in air,
Chasing down dreams that drift without care.
Nature's cupcakes, with frosting divine,
Why hold back when they're all so fine?

Heartbeats of the Garden

Beets and spinach? Not our style,
It's all about berries that make us all smile.
In a garden of giggles, we skip and we race,
Searching for treasures, with joy on our face.

Splat! A squished one gets launched in the sun,
Who knew fruit fights would be so much fun?
It's a splash of nature, on a bright sunny day,
Come join our laughter, let's eat and then play!

Nature's Candy Palette

Sweetness exploding from every branch,
Grab your forks, it's a fruit lover's dance.
Colors collide, a chaotic delight,
Each vibrant piece is a pure appetite.

Giggles erupt as we munch on our finds,
In this garden of flavors, you can lose track of time.
A pie full of wishes, in a crust made of dreams,
Nature serves up laughter, bursting at the seams.

Ripe Reflections

In a garden so lush and bright,
Mischief plays in the soft sunlight.
A strawberry dances, a raspberry twirls,
Inviting giggles from all the girls.

With cherries sitting on top of hats,
Who knew fruits could be such classy cats?
A grape slips down the vine in glee,
Saying, "Join the fun! Come play with me!"

Luscious Labors

Workers dressed in greenish hues,
Pick fruit with such juicy views.
But one slipped on a berry so red,
Now he's got purple juice on his head!

As they laugh and trip in the grove,
An apple jokes, "Let's start a stove!"
For pies that giggle and cakes that squeal,
Who knew such madness could be a meal?

Wandering through Sweetness

A blueberry rolls, what a silly sight,
Chasing a peach that feels just right.
They bump into oranges, cause such a stir,
"Don't squash our fun!" yells the loudest blur.

Bananas in pajamas giggle and sway,
While kiwis don hats and start their ballet.
They spin and they whirl, no time for a frown,
In a fruity parade that takes over the town!

The Fruitful Reverie

In dreams of jam and sweet confetti,
A cantaloupe sings, all bright and petty.
On pancake clouds, the syrup flows,
Giggles erupt as the merriment grows.

With a plunge into cream, they all retreat,
Making the most of this fruity feat.
And when morning comes with a sleepy yawn,
The party's still ripe, just a little drawn.

The Taste of Sunlit Happiness

Joy drips from my lips,
Like sunshine on a toast.
Laughter bounces around,
Sweetness is our host.

Chubby cheeks a-grin,
With snacks that make us dance.
Giggling as we munch,
Who knew fruit could romance?

Each bite a playful tease,
A burst of zest so grand.
I can't help but chuckle,
With sticky, happy hands.

In sunny fields we play,
As nature's song unfolds.
Life's a fruity romp,
Our hearts, a story told.

Chasing the Aromatic Breeze

A scent whirls in the air,
Like a tickle on my nose.
Curious little me,
In search of fruity prose.

I sprint through the orchard,
A giggle on each step.
Who knew that a fruit chase,
Could bring such joy, adept?

The breeze tosses my hair,
While I spot the juicy prize.
With arms stretched wide and loud,
I catch them by surprise!

A feast for silly souls,
We tumble in delight.
Chasing all the flavors,
Such happiness in flight.

Tangy Kisses on My Palate

A tangy smack of joy,
It tickles every taste.
Each bite's a cheeky wink,
No fruit shall go to waste.

With giggles and some juice,
Our faces all aglow.
We munch on bursting bites,
Like kids just stealing dough.

These kisses on my tongue,
Are playful little gibes.
We giggle through the night,
As fruity fun describes.

A rainbow on our plates,
In hues that make us cheer.
Such tangy little joys,
We fill with laughter here.

The Fruitful Symphony of Seasons

Spring sings of sweet delights,
While we dance with our bowls.
The plumper, the better,
For ticklish little souls.

Summer throws a party,
With colors bright and bold.
We gather for the feast,
As laughter takes a hold.

Fall's a chorus of crunch,
As we munch without a care.
Every bite a playful note,
A fruity, friendly affair.

Winter brings the giggles,
With warmth in every hug.
A symphony of seasons,
Wrapped up in all the snug.

Ripe Resplendence

In the garden, fruits collide,
Red and round with seeds inside.
I tried to juggle, but oh dear!
Now I'm splattered, what a smear!

Juicy droplets spinning round,
Giggling loudly, oh what a sound!
My shirt's a canvas, smeared in red,
Not quite the look I'd hoped to spread.

Encounters with Nature

Out in the wild, I made my stand,
With a snack pack in my hand.
A raccoon winked and gave a grin,
I offered him some, his cheeky win!

He snatched a fruit, then took my hat,
I chased him down; what's fun like that?
I must admit - he did look cute,
But not in my clothes, that's simply rude!

The Call of the Orchard

The orchard calls with vibrant hue,
I took a basket, it seemed so true.
But bees had other plans in store,
Their buzzing made me dance and roar!

I plucked a fruit while on the run,
But tripped and tumbled; oh, what fun!
I landed soft, a fruity seat,
With sticky fingers, oh what a treat!

Wandering Zest

Through fields of color, skipping wide,
With sticky hands, I cannot hide.
A splash of juice upon my face,
I looked a wreck, a fruity disgrace!

But laughter bubbled, a joyful sound,
In this messy game, fun is found.
I tumbled, stumbled, rolled so free,
Nature's party, just for me!

Sunkissed Euphoria

In fields where laughter blooms so bright,
I stumbled on a fruit-filled plight.
Sticky fingers, jammed with glee,
Tasting sunshine, oh me, oh me!

A dance of flavors, a pie of cheer,
Tangled treats, we all draw near.
Like acrobats on a sugar spree,
We swing from branches, wild and free!

Wild Harvest Dreams

Once upon a clumsy chase,
I tripped on vines, fell on my face.
Fruits like laughter burst and splat,
Nature's prank, imagine that!

A basket full of silly slips,
Mouths agape with tartest quips.
Picking joy with every stumble,
In this sweet, crazy tumble!

Nectar of the Fields

Bees with giggles buzz and hum,
As nectar flows and taste buds drum.
The flowers wink, it's all a tease,
Come relish in this fruity breeze!

Splattered shirts and silly grins,
We laugh off all our sticky sins.
Sunshine pools in every jar,
A playful feast, we're shining stars!

The Flavorful Labyrinth

In a maze of flavors, oh what fun,
I lost my way, can't tell the sun.
With every turn a tangy chase,
My taste buds dance, my heart's a race!

Strawberry paths and blackberry bends,
Fruity treks, I make amends.
Hiccuping giggles at every twist,
In this wild game, I can't resist!

In the Shade of Ruby Leaves

Underneath the leafy dome,
A fruit parade starts to roam.
Merrily they bounce and jig,
Silly hats on every fig.

Laughter spills from every vine,
As they sip on fizzy brine.
The cherries throw a lively bash,
While raspberries join in with a splash.

Plump blueberries roll down the lane,
Making all the ripened grain.
Giggling gets louder, no chance to cease,
As they dance in joyful peace.

A fruit party, oh what a sight!
Turning day into a night.
In the shade, the mischief grows,
With ruby leaves, the laughter flows.

A Dancer on Sweetened Tongues

Strawberry pirouettes on cream,
Whirling with a foamy dream.
Lemon twirls in zesty flair,
While sugar sprinkles in the air.

A waltz between the cherries bright,
Sipping nectar pure delight.
Grapes giggle, forming ties,
As frosty winds help them fly.

Dancing pairs in fruity glee,
All together, wild and free.
The rhythm calls, they jump and swoon,
Underneath the starlit moon.

Each morsel plays a sweet charade,
In luscious shade, they are displayed.
The dance goes on, a sugary tale,
As laughter fills the fruity trail.

Festooned with Sugar and Sunshine

On a swing of cotton candy,
Lemonade looks oh so dandy.
Sparkling sunbeam shines a light,
As cookies sneak a silly bite.

Cupcakes wear their icing crowns,
Pies are spinning, swapping towns.
Cookies giggle, getting cheeky,
While muffins act a bit too sneaky.

With jellybeans and fruity spritz,
Partying where the sunlight hits.
Every nibble, laughter mixed,
In a world of sweet affixed.

Adventurers of sugarland,
Throwing sprinkles across the strand.
Fun is tied in neon bows,
In the sunshine, joy just flows.

The Scent of Life's Bounty

A whiff of sweetness fills the air,
Bananas laugh without a care.
Peaches wink with juicy cheer,
As melons giggle, drawing near.

The scent of joy, a fragrant spree,
Floats and flutters, wild and free.
Raspberries snicker, play a prank,
While pineapple joins with a merriment rank.

Whirling fragrances, a playful race,
Sun-kissed smiles light up the place.
Each fruit a jester, full of cheer,
Creating harmony far and near.

Savoring aromas, laughter's song,
In a world where we all belong.
Life's sweet bounty, oh what a gift,
In fruity fun, our spirits lift.

Lush Temptations

In the garden, colors bright,
Juicy gems in morning light.
A plump red fruit, oh so sweet,
Can't resist, it's quite the treat!

Friends gather, laughter loud,
Pies baking, they feel proud.
But one bite, they start to stare,
Red juice stains, oh, what a flair!

Splatters here and splatters there,
Wipe your face, it's quite a scare!
Chasing kids, now it's a race,
With sticky hands and a silly face!

Underneath the shady trees,
Silly jokes float on the breeze.
A feast of flavors, life's delight,
Join the fun until the night!

Dancing on the Vine

Berries twirl in a playful way,
Under the sun, they laugh and sway.
Pink and purple, a cheeky sight,
Wiggling around, what a delight!

The bushes giggle, what a fling,
When birds join in and start to sing.
Bouncing ants, they try their dance,
Down the line, they take their chance!

Suddenly, a plop, oh dear!
A juicy berry rolls so near.
Kids start shrieking, gleefully loud,
In this juicy, purple cloud!

As sunset paints the sky so bright,
Berries glow in the soft twilight.
When fun is bursting, laughter divine,
Join the party, dancing on the vine!

The Taste of Nostalgia

Remember days with carefree glee?
Crispy leaves and a big oak tree.
Pockets stuffed with little sweets,
Running wild on summer streets!

Tasting treats from grandmas' hands,
Wobbly chairs, filled with berry bands.
Sticky fingers, happy sighs,
Memories found in every bite!

In the kitchen, flour flies high,
Mixing fun – oh my, oh my!
The jam is spreading, oh what fun,
We'll gobble it all before we're done!

Drenched in sunlight, laughter rings,
Every taste takes flight on wings.
Past and present, sweet embrace,
In the flavors, we find our place.

A Symphony of Flavors

Notes of sweetness fill the air,
Fruits compose a tuneful fare.
Plucked from nature's vibrant song,
Each bite sings, you won't go wrong!

Lemon plays a zesty tune,
Joined by berries under the moon.
The crunch of joy, the splash of cream,
Together they create a dream!

Spoon here, scoop there, such a mess,
Tasting fortune, pure success.
Dancing flavors, round and round,
Finding laughter in every sound!

So grab a plate, join in the cheer,
Let's gather close and shed the fear.
In this mix, we find our fun,
A festival for everyone!

Savoring the Summer's Harvest

In the garden, a riotous spree,
Cherries giggle, ripe for thee.
Blueberries burst with a giggly grin,
While raspberries argue which one to win.

A basket wobble, near my feet,
Strawberries dancing, oh what a treat!
Lemonade stands cheerfully call,
My tongue twirls like a carnival ball.

Whirls of Wild Flavors and Colors

Jellybeans in shades, a sight so bright,
Plums and peaches joining the plight.
Grapes hang in bunches, having a ball,
Tasting one's risky – will I drop them all?

Tarts sashay, sweet on my plate,
Who knew a fruit could tempt fate?
Mangoes waltz with a wink and a laugh,
While kiwis plot a juicy staff.

Everlasting Taste of Childhood

Grandma's kitchen, a fruity delight,
Cheesecake parties that last through the night.
Pineapples giggle, peaches blush,
In the sweet soup of nostalgic hush.

Sprinkles of joy, a dash of cheer,
Lollipops laughing, drawing us near.
In a world where taste buds can play,
Each bite's an adventure, come what may.

Mirth of the Orchard

Under the trees, a fruity parade,
Cider so fizzy, the joy never fade.
Apples in jests, they tumble and roll,
While nuts whisper secrets, losing control.

Carts filled with laughter, big and small,
Each crunch a giggle, oh what a ball!
Fruit snacks in pockets, sticky delight,
Sharing this whimsy feels just right.

Sweet Juices of Dawn

Morning sun spills on the ground,
A dance of flavors all around.
In the fridge, a jumbled feast,
Who knew fruit could be a beast?

Stumbling thoughts and sticky hands,
A smoothie job that barely stands.
Blenders roar like hungry bears,
As splatters fly and fill the air.

Limes join in, a zesty crew,
With lemons squawking, "Let's break through!"
Oh, quirky fruits, you make me grin,
Let's squeeze and squish, let fun begin!

So grab that bowl, don't you delay,
A fruity mess might rule the day.
With giggles shared, we toast with glee,
To crazy mornings, wild and free.

Whispers of the Wild Vines

Creeping tendrils in the sun,
A leafy dance, oh what a fun!
Grapes are gossiping in the breeze,
Whispering secrets behind the trees.

Strawberries wear their polka dots,
Cherries laugh in merry knots.
Blackberries hide in thorny zones,
While raspberries toss their sassy tones.

The wild vines twist and twirl,
With fruits that leap and spin and whirl.
Each bite a giggle, each sip a cheer,
A silly shout, "More fruit, we cheer!"

In fields of laughter, we'll collect,
These whimsical wonders, a sweet effect.
Joy spills forth, like juice so bright,
As laughter guides us through the night.

Nectar Dripped from Sun-Kissed Boughs

In orchard shade, a juicy drop,
Plump fruit just waits for you to plop.
With sticky fingers and rosy cheeks,
Each one's a treasure, a sweet mystique.

Peaches giggle, so soft and round,
Quick to start rolling on the ground.
Plums compete with a bounce and flip,
In this fruity carnival, let's take a trip!

Melons boast of sweetness bold,
While coconuts act oh-so-old.
"Crack me open!" the papayas plead,
With fruity antics, they take the lead.

So fill your basket, grab a spoon,
Chomp and gobble 'neath the moon.
These sun-kissed gems will make you laugh,
In a world where fruits do write their path.

Serenade of Crimson Fruits

Crimson treasures on the vine,
Match the laughter, oh so fine.
Ripe tomatoes singing sweet,
Playful songs that can't be beat.

Watermelons clad in green,
Shouting jokes, oh what a scene!
With every slice, a juice-filled cheer,
Let's celebrate all fruits we hold dear.

Raspberries rap a funny tune,
Mangoes slide under the moon.
Each fruity giggle echoes loud,
Join the dance, come, be proud!

The party's here, don't miss a beat,
With frolicsome fruits, life's a treat.
So grab a fruit, give it a whirl,
In this sweet serenade, let joy unfurl!

Eden's Palate

In a garden lush and bright,
Fruits dance in the soft, warm light.
An apple winks, a peach declares,
'We're the snacks with juicy flares!'

A cherry giggles, plump and round,
While kiwis hide beneath the ground.
Pineapples wear their crowns so proud,
While bananas cheer, 'We're fruity loud!'

Grapes hang tight with giggly glee,
Singing tunes of jubilee.
They swing from vines, a wobbly show,
In this fruit fest, they steal the show!

So come and taste this fruity fate,
Where every bite's a joyful date.
In Eden's arms, we laugh and munch,
Fruit lovers unite for a sweet punch!

Radiant Offerings

A platter stacked with colors bright,
Each fruit a beacon, pure delight.
Lemons shout with zesty cheer,
While berries wave their hands in fear!

'Catch me if you can!' a melon croons,
As citrus dance to summer tunes.
A kiwi laughs in silly rhyme,
'You can't resist my fuzzy clime!'

The oranges roll, a bright parade,
While apples caught in games are played.
Peaches blush and giggle too,
In this feast, a merry crew!

With each sweet bite, a burst of fun,
Radiant joy for everyone.
A carousel of taste and jest,
In this fruit world, we're all blessed!

Nightingale's Snack

As nightingale sings soft and sweet,
He pecks at snacks, his favorite treat.
Raspberries tease, 'We're quite the catch!'
While strawberries boast, 'You'll never match!'

A pineapple swings, bold and grand,
Tempting birds from the upper land.
'Hey, don't forget my fresh delight!'
'Join the feast, sing through the night!'

Mangoes twirl in the moonlit glow,
While dew drops cheer, 'Let's steal the show!'
With laughter ringing in the air,
The hungry tune becomes a flare!

So let the nightingale take a bow,
In this fruity snack-filled town.
With every peck and every sip,
We raise a toast to this wild trip!

A Chorus of Fruits

Gather round, the fruits unite,
In a chorus, oh what a sight!
They sing with joy, a fruity song,
Keeping rhythm all night long!

Berries chirp their shiny notes,
While apples harmonize with quotes.
Bananas sway, their peels a-blur,
And oranges join in with a purr!

Grapefruits sip their tangy tea,
Peaches laugh, 'Come dance with me!'
The coconuts bang their shells so loud,
In this fruity band, we're all so proud!

As they jive under the moon's sweet dome,
This fruity choir feels like home.
So let the music never cease,
In this charming, merry feast!

The Sweets of Autumn

In a basket so bright, those fruits all around,
Chubby little packages, sweet on the ground.
I tripped on a pumpkin, fell right on my face,
But laughter's the rule in this fruity place.

Apples in costumes, wearing hats made of sprout,
Dancing with acorns, they sing and they shout.
A pear with a mustache, so proud and so round,
Claims he's the king, in this whimsical town.

Plums wear their purple coats, clever and sly,
While cherries throw raves, twirling up to the sky.
"Come taste our sweet jam! It's totally fab!"
I say, as I stumble on my own fruit-lab.

So grab a sweet snack, don't think twice, just munch,
And giggle with friends over a sweet fruit lunch.
With laughter and juice, it's a vibrant parade,
Autumn's silly treats make blissfully fun escapade.

Glittering Treats

Oh glittering wonders, where sweetness abounds,
With icing that twinkles and joy that surrounds.
Cupcakes in tiaras, they pounce and they play,
Shouting, "Eat us quick, or we'll run away."

Marshmallows giggle, in a cocoa-filled bowl,
They float like a dream, taking over with roll.
The sprinkles, now wild, are a colorful crew,
Jumping on pastries, like kids do at the zoo!

Chocolate is dancing, oh what a delight,
With caramel twirls, they're a wondrous sight.
Donuts in pajamas, lounging with flair,
They whisper sweet secrets, with frosting to share.

So munch and be merry, join this silly feast,
With treats that bring giggles, never the least.
In this land of sweet chaos, we revel and cheer,
For glittering treats bring us all lots of cheer!

Dreamy Fruit Pies

In the land of pie dreams, where fruit does collide,
A crusty enchantress puts flavor inside.
Peaches in pajamas, singing a song,
"Who knew we could dance? Come join us, be strong!"

Cherries are tiny, with wands made of twist,
They sprinkle their magic, you don't want to miss.
Blueberries giggle, dressed in shades of blue,
While raspberries whisper, "We're cuter than you!"

The pies take a vote, who's the best in the batch?
With flour in jackets, they all look to hatch.
They bake up a ruckus, in unison chime,
"Let's pie the whole world, one slice at a time!"

So revel in flavors, and smile with delight,
With every sweet bite, there's a comical sight.
In crunchy delight, let your laughter arise,
For life's just a party in dreamy fruit pies.

Fabric of Sweetness

In a quilt made of sugar, stitched neat with delight,
Endless swirls of candy, all dancing at night.
Cotton candy clouds float, all sugar and fluff,
While chocolate chip kittens say, "We're cute enough!"

They stitch up the seams with giggles and glee,
For every sweet flavor is a sight to see.
Waffles do waltzes, with strawberries bold,
While syrupy rainbows are stories retold.

A donut's round belly, so soft and so grand,
Claims it can flap, with a cake-happy band.
Soda pop twirls, making bubbles that sing,
Each sip is a laugh; oh, the joy that it brings!

So wear your sweet patchwork, flaunt every bite,
In this fabric of sweetness, let's dance through the night.
With flavors colliding, and fun ever near,
In a world full of giggles, we'll spread all the cheer.

Velvet and Vines

In the garden, fruits take a dive,
Their colors clash, oh how they strive!
One plump grape claims he's the best,
While the raspberries laugh, never distressed.

A strawberry prances with a grand flair,
Saying he's royalty, without a care.
But a blueberry winks, with purple glee,
"Dance with me, friends, let's all just be!"

The beetroot sighed, feeling quite shy,
"Why can't I join in? I'm not that dry!"
But the others just chuckled, without a frown,
"You're more of a veggie, time to sit down!"

So they partied on, while the sun was bright,
Adding laughter to each glorious bite!
In a world of laughter and sunny delight,
The garden's a stage, under its light!

The Hidden Orchard

In a secret grove, where fruits collide,
A pear told a tale of juicy pride.
"I'm smooth and luscious, can't you see?"
The apple just chuckled, said, "Not quite me!"

"A mischievous plum rolled by in a flash,
Spilling his secrets, oh what a bash!"
The cherry piped up, with a wink and a grin,
"I'm the sweetest snack, let the fun begin!"

The oranges laughed, with zest for life,
"We'll mix it up, stir joy, avoid strife!"
But the lemons just pouted, somewhat sour,
"We'll bring the zing, just hand us the power!"

As the sun set low, shadows danced around,
In this hidden orchard, joy knows no bound.
They feasted on jokes, flavors so bright,
In the orchard of giggles, everything's right!

Taste of Tomorrow

Future flavors swirled in a bowl,
Scrumptious delights, so good for the soul.
A kiwi stood tall, dreaming of fame,
"Just wait for my smoothie, they'll know my name!"

Grumpy old lemon said, "Not quite today,
Wait till they try me, then I'll have my say!"
But the mango was smooth, with a wink of the eye,
"Let them all taste, I'm the fruit to fly!"

Silly blueberries jumped in a dance,
While the cherries debated their chances for romance.
But every bite sparkled with flavors anew,
As they crafted their dreams, a colorful brew!

Tomorrow arrived with a splash and a grin,
Fruit salads were made, let the laughter spin!
With zest in the air, they savored the play,
In a whirl of delight, they welcomed the day!

Sweetness in the Breeze

On a windy path, sweets drifted by,
Marshmallow clouds made a fluffy sky.
The lilac bushes giggled with bliss,
"Let's dance with the wind, we won't let it miss!"

A frisky fig swung by on a leaf,
Sharing wild secrets, exposing the chief.
The juicy berries bounced, quite in a funk,
"You call us fruit? We're more like a punk!"

They spun in circles, creating a whirl,
Daring the clouds to give them a twirl.
"Lemonade rivers can't hold us quite still,
We're a juicy crew, we're chasing the thrill!"

The breeze carried laughter through branches up high,
As they juggled with flavors, oh my, oh my!
In this frolicsome world of sweetness true,
Laughter's the flavor, and fun's the view!

Shades of Crimson

A fruit that stains your shirt so red,
You chase the juice, like it's a dread.
With every squish, a laugh does pop,
Who knew a snack could make you hop?

Stumbling over laughter, oh what a scene,
You trip on your giggles, and it seems so mean.
A tart like a joke, it bites but with grace,
And leaves you grinning all over your face.

In bowls of chaos, they scatter and play,
A tug of war where you lose the day.
With friends around, it's a fruit buffet,
And lip-smacking fun is here to stay!

So, grab a handful, or maybe three,
Just watch your step, don't trip on glee.
These shades of crimson bring silly delight,
In the taste of childhood, we'll party all night.

Essence of Abundance

A garden bursting, colors collide,
You reach for the sweetness, let joy be your guide.
But hit a patch that's extra gooey,
Your fingers stuck—oh boy, how chewy!

Bouncing about, we gather the crew,
To munch on mischief, there's plenty to chew.
With every bite, a squirt, a shout,
Who knew a fruit could cause such a rout?

The baskets overflow, can't carry a thing,
Like ants with candy, we just want to cling.
But sticky situations, they make us laugh,
As we scale the tower of our fruity craft!

With spoons in hand, we create our art,
A ridiculous feast, straight from the heart.
So here's to the sweetness, chaos galore,
In essence of fun, we're always wanting more!

Whimsy and Whispers

A plump little fruit, with giggles that burst,
Whispers of sweetness, a candy-like thirst.
We reach for the basket, our arms in a twist,
Stuck in a frenzy, can't resist this tryst!

In the chaos of color, we bounce and we sway,
As juice flows like laughter, come join the play.
A pluck and a munch—a wonderful sound,
We're creating a mess, spinning round and round.

The mischief we make, it drips and it splats,
Sticky-faced children, wearing fruity hats.
A comedy show with each bite we take,
Oh, what a riot; life's a laugh and a cake!

So gather your pals for this edible glee,
In the fruit-splattered madness, we feel so free.
With whimsy in hearts, we wander and roam,
In each juicy moment, we build our own home.

The Taste of the Earth

Digging through dirt for a prize that shines,
What a wild chase for these wrinkled finds!
With earthy delights, we munch on the fun,
And giggle like children, our laughter's begun.

The taste of the earth, oh so bold,
A splash of sweet chaos never grows old.
"We're fruit ninjas!" we laugh as we dash,
Navigating the mess, a juicy splash!

From pies to the palate, we savor and scoff,
Each bite a prank waiting for the soft cough.
With sticky fingers and laughter that grows,
In the garden of whimsy, anything goes!

So raise up your hands for this glorious mess,
In the taste of the earth, we're truly blessed.
With ripe, juicy giggles and smiles ear to ear,
We celebrate joy, bringing everyone near!

A Feast for the Senses

In the garden, colors clash,
Fruits are dancing, oh what a splash!
Strawberries sing, in a juicy parade,
While blueberries giggle, not afraid.

Leaves are whispering sweet little lies,
About the treasure hidden in pies.
Raspberries, oh, the mischievous jest,
Invite ants to join their fruity fest!

Yogurt joins the party, looking so grand,
Spilling out laughter, quite unplanned.
Spoons are ready, the feast will commence,
But who will get the last drop of essence?

So raise your glass of punch for a cheer,
To all our fruits, let's give a loud jeer!
With every bite, let the humor ignite,
Join the fun, it's a wild fruity night!

The Aroma of Juiceness

The kitchen smells, oh what a delight,
Caught in a war of flavor and flight.
Peach cobbler singing with a sugary song,
While bananas tease, saying, 'You're doing it wrong!'

Rusty old blender grumbles in strife,
Creating a chaos, oh what a life!
Fruits in a frenzy, they whirl and they grind,
A smoothie of laughter, refreshingly blind.

The juice spills over, making a scene,
Dance of colors; it's quite the routine!
But who could have guessed, in all this fun,
That the cat would join in, and steal the pun?

So gather 'round, it's a juicy affair,
With sticky fingers and fruity flair.
Let's raise our cups filled with sweet, silly glee,
As we toast to this wild food jubilee!

Threads of Summer Sun

Golden rays weave through the trees,
As watermelon splashes, it's sure to please.
Cherries are laughing, hanging so low,
While peaches play dress-up, putting on a show.

Garden gnomes cheer with their silly grins,
As fruit flies debate where the party begins.
Nectarines squeeze in for a closer view,
While the sun tickles squishy grapes in blue.

Picnics await with ants on parade,
Apples in hats, what a fruity charade!
Each slice tells stories of summer's bright kiss,
As everyone giggles at nature's pure bliss.

So let's roll out the blanket, don't delay,
And devour the magic before it goes away.
With laughter and juice, let's savor the fun,
In this threaded tale of the summer sun!

Nature's Bounty Unfolded

Out in the woods, we hear nature's tune,
Berries are shouting, 'Come eat us soon!
Elderflowers giggle, swaying in glee,
While squirrels conspire, it's a fruity spree.

Muffins are baking, with cream on the side,
Bananas and muffins share joy as they slide.
All in a row, fruits line up for fun,
Singing sweet songs 'til the day is done.

Raspberries wear crowns made of crumbly fluff,
Daring the others to say, 'That's enough!'
Lemons roll over, making quite a fuss,
Zesty and sassy, they join in the bus.

So grab a plate, let the laughter unfold,
Nature provides us with blessings untold.
With giggles and crunches, let's savor each bite,
In this fun fruit tale, the world feels just right!

The Language of Ripeness

In the sun, we squish and squeal,
Fruits so ripe, it's a big deal.
They giggle softly on the vine,
Complaining, 'Hey, I'm feeling fine!'

Juicy jokes in every bite,
Puns are ripe, it's pure delight.
They whisper secrets, oh so sweet,
Just try to catch them—what a feat!

Tomatoes blush beside the greens,
Radishes hiding behind the scenes.
'I'm a fruit!' one cucumber gripes,
As lettuce shudders and rolls its stripes.

Grapes get tangled, giggle and roll,
Making wine dreams, that's their goal.
But watch your step, they'll pop and stain,
A fruity dance, it's not mundane!

Harvest Harmonies

In the fields, a tune begins,
As corn and beans laugh in spins.
The pumpkins party, round and bright,
'We're the snacks for Halloween night!'

Cherries chat, they're quite the crowd,
While apples shout, 'We're very proud!'
The raspberries fight for the spotlight,
Their jokes are funny, they're a delight!

Carrots hum a crunching song,
While beetroots argue, 'Who's not wrong?'
Fruits in chorus, a sight to see,
Nature's jesters, wild and free.

Lemons squeeze out puns so sour,
Limes join in, it's their finest hour.
Together they share laughter burst,
For fruity fun is always first!

Refreshing Reveries

Beneath a tree, we laugh and play,
Fruits take over, what a display!
Strawberries dance with every gust,
In this party, we simply trust.

On the table, snacks galore,
They argue over who's the score.
'I'm the sunniest!' a peach will claim,
While pears play hide and seek with fame.

Watermelons laugh, 'We're the best,'
In juicy slices, they'll jest.
As elders roll their eyes in jest,
Saying, 'Who knew fruit could be a fest?'

Kiwi cracks a pun so bold,
As fruity tales are slowly told.
In refreshing dreams, they bounce about,
Silly smiles, laughter, no doubt!

Orchard Echoes

In orchards bright, the whispers sound,
As fruits collide upon the ground.
Cherries chuckle, apples grin,
'We're the best, let's pull you in!'

Grapefruit groans, 'I'm too tart today,'
While juicy oranges laugh away.
'Join the fun, it's quite a treat,'
As they foam up a zesty feat!

Season's end brings silly cheer,
Pumpkins boast, their time is here.
As winter aims to take a bow,
They giggle softly, 'Not yet, wow!'

In this Echo, voices play,
Fruits and laughs, in sweet dismay.
With every bite, a silent cheer,
For fruity fun, it's crystal clear!

Nature's Lush Confection

In the garden, joy does bloom,
Where laughter chases away the gloom.
Cherries giggle on the vine,
While raspberries read a funny sign.

Bumblebees buzz with a comedic twist,
Tickling petals in a fruit-filled mist.
Strawberries wear the silliest hats,
Prancing around like chubby acrobats.

Lemonade spills, a soury fate,
As kids chase after, think it's great.
They trip and tumble, laughter loud,
While the fruit hangs heavy, oh so proud.

In this fruity realm, smiles ignite,
As nature serves laughs, pure delight.
Join the fun, don't you dare miss,
In this candy garden filled with bliss!

Radiant Hues of Late Harvest

October leaves are turning bright,
As apples prank each other by night.
Pumpkins chuckle, their orange skin,
While squirrels tease, attempting to grin.

Grapes wear sunglasses, oh what a show,
While pie recipes begin to flow.
Cranberries jump in the crisp cool air,
Wearing little scarves, what a flair!

The orchard's alive with a playful chase,
As wind carries scents of sweet embrace.
Kids get sticky, laughter does soar,
As each fruit offers more and more.

In the fun of hues both vivid and vast.
Nature's harvest, a riotous blast!
Come join the antics, take a seat,
And dance with the fruits, oh, what a treat!

Fables of the Fruiting Grove

Once was a fig with a tale to tell,
Of a mishap that went quite well.
He slipped on dew, a slippery ride,
And landed in a jelly jar, inside!

Bananas laughed till they turned a shade,
As word of his squishy fate was made.
With whipped cream clouds, they danced in glee,
Creating stories that tickled the tree.

Peaches blushed as the gossip spread,
Of blueberries telling tall tales instead.
A fruit parade, so quirky and grand,
Where humor reigns in the sunny land.

So gather round, let the laughter flow,
In this grove where the wild tales grow.
Each fruit a friend, with anecdotes to share,
An orchard of joy, beyond compare!

Velvet Red in the Golden Light

Under the sun, they glisten and glow,
Velvet fruits ready for a fun show.
Raspberry mischief is brewing nearby,
As they practice acrobatics to fly!

A bouquet of cherries chase a swift breeze,
While ladybugs laugh with delightful ease.
Watermelons giggle, their seeds in a race,
Creating curious patterns all over the place.

The pomegranates gossip, plump and so round,
With tales of sweet dramas that know no bounds.
In this realm, where silliness thrives,
Fruitful hilarity keeps joy alive.

So join the riot, embrace the fun,
In this glistening harvest, laughter's begun!
With every bite of laughter to spread,
Life is juicier, go ahead, be fed!

Golden Hours of the Grove

In the grove, the fruits all grin,
A cheery place, where smiles begin.
They dance and jiggle, oh so round,
Nature's laughter, a joyful sound.

Squirrels skitter, they play their tricks,
Chasing behind, those tiny picks.
With every munch, they squeak and squeal,
Sharing secrets, that's the deal!

The sun's a jester in the trees,
Tickling leaves with a teasing breeze.
Laughter bubbles in the air,
The grove's a stage, with fun to spare!

So come along, don't be a bore,
Join the fun, let's spread some more.
With every bite, let giggles flow,
In this golden hour, let joy grow!

Serendipity of the Seasons

Spring's a trickster, blooms anew,
Blushing colors, vibrant view.
Summer's laughter, bright and loud,
Dancing freely, oh so proud!

Autumn's crunch, a playful tease,
Leaves like confetti, rustle with ease.
Winter giggles in a soft snow,
Wraps around us, like a warm glow.

Each season swirls, a comic show,
They slip and slide, then steal the show.
Jokes in the wind, and laughter bright,
Nature's rhythm—a sheer delight!

So let's toast to each zany turn,
With every season, there's much to learn.
In nature's jest, we find our cheer,
Embrace the fun throughout the year.

Nature's Secret Lullaby

Whispers drift from trees so fine,
Crickets' chirps, a soft design.
The moonlight giggles on the grass,
As sleepy critters wander past.

A raccoon hums a silly tune,
While fireflies prance below the moon.
They twirl and glide, such playful sights,
In this hush, the joy ignites.

Hedgerow rustles with cheeky glee,
Nature's joke, a wild jubilee.
With every sigh and gentle breeze,
A laughter wrapped in leaves and trees.

So let dreams soar on softest wings,
In nighttime's arms, where laughter sings.
Embrace the night's sweet, playful art,
Nature's lullaby warms the heart!

The Color of Juices

Purple pops with a playful spin,
Strawberry red laughs from within.
Orange giggles, oh so bright,
Each drop dances in the light.

Juices swirl in a crazy mess,
Cups overflow, it's pure excess!
With every splash, they sing a rhyme,
A fruity party, just in time.

Pineapple winks, a tropical tease,
Lime joins in, with jolts and wheezes.
Together blending, a cheerful brew,
What a riot, a colorful view!

So raise a glass, let laughter soar,
Taste the wild—there's fun galore!
In every sip, joy does reside,
Come share the laughter, let's abide!

Harvest Moon and Juicy Dreams

Under the moon, the fruits do dance,
With their laughter, they take a chance.
Squished between fingers, they giggle and tease,
A juicy joke carried on the breeze.

In a pie or a jam, they put on a show,
Wobbling about, trying not to grow.
Pies with faces, they roll and they bounce,
Each slice a chuckle, just waiting to flounce.

Late-night snacks that make you grin,
A tug at your heart, let the fun begin!
Syrupy drizzles, they know how to charm,
With a laugh and a wink, they mean no harm.

As stars twinkle bright, the fruits wave goodbye,
With a wink and a nod, they bid you to try.
Harvest the joy, in each bite you'll find,
A world full of giggles, all fruit, no grind!

A Gastronomic Summer's Embrace

Summer's here with a splash and a flop,
Fruits at the market, oh, what a crop!
Strawberries singing, 'Eat us with glee!'
In a salad with greens, or plain, just for me.

Munching away, I try not to giggle,
As juice dribbles down with each silly wiggle.
Cherries wearing hats, they play hide and seek,
A fruity embrace, where flavors peak.

Think of the flavors, oh what a sight,
Tasting a rainbow, what pure delight!
Watermelon smiles, so big and bright,
Each juicy bite is a burst of pure light.

When summer bids farewell with a sigh,
Fruits chuckle softly, 'Oh, we'll fly high!'
In pies or in dreams, they'll never be late,
In laughter and joy, they'll always be great!

Lullabies of Ripe Red Orbs

Night falls gently, the fruits hum a tune,
Under the glow of the grinning moon.
Crimson orbs sway on branches that creak,
Singing sweet lullabies, oh so unique.

They dream of desserts, of jam and parfait,
While seeds in their dreams dance and play.
'Don't squish us too hard, we might burst!' they croon,
Get ready for laughter, it's fruit festooned!

In baskets they giggle, piled high with cheer,
Better grab a fork, oh dear, oh dear!
Each bright little fruit a story to tell,
With a wink and a nod, it's a juicy swell.

As night draws near, they sweetly conspire,
To twist and to tangle, send taste buds higher.
With each little bite, joy's over the moon,
Under the stars, their laughter's in tune!

Fields of Flavorful Indulgence

In fields so vibrant, where laughter's a must,
Fruits frolic freely, collecting their dust.
Each berry a clown, in colors so bright,
Rolling with humor, such a sweet sight!

Raspberry jokes that make everyone grin,
Blueberries bouncing, with chuckles within.
'Pick me, pick me!' they all start to shout,
As baskets fill up, there's never a doubt.

Plum pudding parties, with cakes on the side,
Fruits play their cards, they take it in stride.
Juicy confessions, come take a big bite,
Where sweetness and laughter fit perfectly right.

As harvest draws near, with a wink and a sway,
Fruits promise joy, in every display.
With giggles galore, and smiles all around,
In fields of indulgence, pure fun can be found!

Echoes of Orchard Laughs

In the orchard, a fruit goes pop,
A mischievous laugh from the top.
Bouncing on branches, a plump little chap,
Hiding from squirrels, doing a snap!

Under the sun, they roll around,
With giggles and wiggles, they dance on ground.
Juice stains the shirt of a lad so spry,
Chasing cheeky thieves that leap and fly.

Here comes the rain, and they start to glide,
Slipping and sliding, oh what a ride!
A tumble of color right under the tree,
Nature's confetti for you and me.

The sun dips low, the fruits say cheers,
Whispers of laughter echo through years.
With each little bite, a joke finds its way,
In this fruity kingdom, it's always play day!

Sunkissed Bliss in Nature's Palette

Under the sun, they wear their hues,
Strawberry reds and blueberry blues.
With squishy giggles and sugary sighs,
They lurk in the fields under open skies.

A raspberry nibbles on a leaf so neat,
While a blackberry tickles its tiny feet.
'Hey there, friend! Come join my spree.'
They skate down the hill, in pure melody.

Juice-sprinkled laughter, a sticky delight,
A dance on the grass, what a funny sight!
With hats made of leaves and shoes made of sun,
It's a fruit-themed party; oh, what fun!

As dusk sets in, they twinkle and twirl,
While crickets and critters begin to swirl.
In this fruity fiesta, mischief prevails,
With stories of giggles told in the trails!

Secrets of the Thicket: A Flavor Tale

In the deep thicket, mischief brews,
Nibbly critters with berry shoes.
Whispers of flavor rise up to play,
Shyly hiding in their leafy array.

A nectar thief with a snarky grin,
Trots through the bushes, ready to win.
'Catch me if you can!' it snickers out loud,
While the fruits roll over, part of the crowd.

With a splash of juice and a dash of charm,
They frolic in fields, no cause for alarm.
Bouncing like bubbles on a bright summer day,
Making up stories and foolish ballet.

The secrets they keep, oh – what a delight!
In this thicket hide-and-seek, day turns to night.
A serenade of flavors, sweet and absurd,
Nature's own comedians, how they've stirred!

Festive Jams and Runaway Pies

A pie on the table, just came to life,
With a wink and a nudge, it causes a strife.
'Me first!' yells a jam, all glistening bright,
As they plot their escape in the still of the night.

With plump little poofs, they leap and they roll,
A vintage dance at sweet harvest's toll.
'Last one to the picnic is a moldy crust!'
They race through the grass, it's a fruity must!

Berries with giggles and pastries surreal,
Creating a ruckus with each fruity meal.
A tangle of laughter, crusts fluttering high,
In a festival frenzy, oh me, oh my!

So grab a slice, join their whimsical spree,
These runaway treats are just wild and free.
With every sweet bite, a riotous cheer,
In this carnival of flavors, there's no room for fear!

Pulses of the Garden

In the garden, plants do sway,
With tomatoes on holiday.
Peas whisper, 'We're quite the charm!'
Though one just rolled off the farm!

Radishes wear a feisty grin,
'Who knew we could be such a win?'
Lettuce leaves in a jolly dance,
While onions try to steal a glance!

Carrots giggle in the mud,
Saying, 'We're not just a dud!'
Cucumbers, sly, then hide away,
'Pick us later, it's our play!'

Gasping greens, in shouts of glee,
'Join us here for a veggie tea!'
Fruits apply for the gardening role,
But they roll out, losing their stroll!

Dances with June

June comes in with colors bright,
Fruits in tow, oh what a sight!
Strawberries twirl in frosty caps,
Marmalade dreams in sunny laps!

Raspberries laugh saying, 'Look at me!'
As they decorate the jamberrée.
Dancing late under the moon,
With fruity friends, it's quite the tune!

Blueberries jive, a lively crew,
Flinging juice like morning dew.
Kiwi spins, a fuzzy flare,
While lemons pout, 'It's just not fair!'

Peaches tease with velvety skin,
'Who needs a gym when you spin?!'
Plums proclaim, 'Come join our quest!'
For this fruity fiesta, you'll be blessed!

Harvesting Joy

In the field, the work begins,
With laughter shared and fruity sins.
Apple baskets overflow wide,
While pears just grin, full of pride!

Tangerines play hide and seek,
'Don't pick us yet, it's still peak!'
Grapes complain, 'We're squished in here!'
But dance away, with no fear!

Pineapples wear crowns on their heads,
While fruits declare their harvest spreads.
Limes make faces, full of sass,
Say, 'When life gives you fruit, have a blast!'

Ready for pies or jams to brew,
Smiles blossom, all shiny and new.
Fruits unite in a tasty cheer,
Harvesting joy the whole year!

Chasing Flavors

Chasing flavors, folks do sprint,
Ripe fruits whisper, 'Take a hint!'
Bananas slide on kitchen floors,
While cherries sneak out through the doors!

Honeydew hides, what a sneak!
Saying, 'Catch me if you seek!'
Mangoes leap in the fruit bowl,
While guavas rock 'n' roll!

Coconuts clash, full of might,
Saying, 'Crack us open, what a sight!'
Pomegranates burst with glee,
'We're the party, can't you see?'

Watermelons join the crew,
Slurping juice, what fun to do!
Chasing flavors, what a race,
Every bite's a happy place!

Harvest Moon Serenade

Under the moon, we twirl and dance,
With giggles like berries, a silly prance.
The harvest's here, it's quite a sight,
Plump little fruits, oh what a night!

Chubby cheeks and laughter loud,
We form a most ridiculous crowd.
With sticky fingers and silly grins,
Who knew fruit picking could lead to sins?

Splat goes the pie, right on my face,
In this delightful, fruity race.
The stars above wink in delight,
As we stumble home, all through the night!

So here's to the moon, and laughter too,
In fields of fruit, we find our cue.
With each silly moment, our hearts ignite,
Under the harvest moon, it's pure delight!

Petals and Purple Hues

In the garden, where chaos reigns,
Petals dance like little trains.
Purple smudges everywhere,
We laugh and roll without a care.

Funky hats and muddy shoes,
Trying to pick without the blues.
A squished one here, a splash of juice,
Oh, it seems we're quite the loose!

Bumblebees buzzing, join our song,
In this patch, we can't go wrong.
Launching fruits like cannonballs,
Laughter echoes off the walls!

So let's create our fruity mess,
In petals soft, we'll find our jest.
With every chuckle, we break the rules,
Our garden party, for all the fools!

Sun-Kissed Delights

Under the sun, we start our race,
Chasing shadows, it's a wild chase.
Jars of jam, what a sticky sight,
Each spoonful brings pure delight!

With sunhats askew, we make a stand,
Dropping fruits straight from our hand.
Splatters of sunshine on our clothes,
Bees buzzing, oh how it glows!

The taste-test leads to silly faces,
As everyone claims their fruity paces.
From jam to jelly, chaos ensues,
Our kitchen's a whirlwind of fruity blues!

So grab a spoon and join the fun,
Together we'll splatter, there's no need to run.
As the sun dips down and the day takes flight,
We'll laugh our hearts out 'til the night!

Secrets of the Orchard

In the orchard, we hatch our plots,
Searching for fruits in crooked spots.
Sneaky smiles and whispers low,
Who can find the best, we'll show!

Apples bounce and pears take flight,
In this game of pure delight.
Watch your step, don't trip on hay,
Or you'll end up in a fruity fray!

A sudden splash, a plop and a laugh,
Fruits are slippery, take a gaffe!
With our baskets full, we feast tonight,
But watch those pies; oh, what a sight!

So here's to secrets in orchards spread,
Where laughter blooms and joy is fed.
With every bite, our spirits sway,
In this playful game, we'll forever play!

www.ingramcontent.com/pod-product-compliance
Lightning Source LLC
Chambersburg PA
CBHW060141230426
43661CB00003B/518